WOLVES

WOLVES

A Stunning Glimpse into Nature's Hunters in the Wild

Tom Jackson

amber
BOOKS

Copyright © 2019 Amber Books Ltd.

Published by Amber Books Ltd
United House
North Road
London N7 9DP
United Kingdom
www.amberbooks.co.uk
Instagram: amberbooksltd
Facebook: www.facebook.com/amberbooks
Twitter: @amberbooks

Project Editor: Sarah Uttridge
Design: Keren Harragan
Picture Research: Terry Forshaw

ISBN: 978-1-78274-768-0

Printed in China

4 6 8 10 9 7 5 3

Contents

Introduction

The wolf occupies a very special place in our hearts and minds, so much so that it is a regular character in myths and fables, and it remains a powerful symbol of savagery, cunning and danger. No other creature commands the same mix of admiration, fear, loathing and love as this biggest of wild dog species. That admiration is for the wolf's physical abilities and social nature, which reflects

our own. The fear comes from the wolf's strength, speed and intelligence, which makes it one of nature's most effective killers, especially when working in a team. The loathing and love both arrived through our two species' long shared history. The wolf's killer instincts frequently put it into direct conflict with shepherds and herdsmen for whom the beast is an eternal foe. At the same time, wolves, or at least their tamed descendants, are welcomed into our homes as much-loved pets and members of the family. This book reveals the wolf, an enduring enigma of nature, red in tooth and claw.

ABOVE:
The wolf lives in a strict social hierarchy, and every dog knows its place – or is quickly reminded of it when it oversteps its position.

OPPOSITE:
A noble hunter, and a highly mobile one to boot, the grey wolf is a born survivor.

The Lone Wolf

For the best part of the last 100,000 years, the wolf was the world's most abundant large predator and the most widespread land mammal on the planet. The wolf had its physiology to thank for this dominance. The dog anatomy deploys a lightweight and long-legged frame along with a large lung capacity and powerful jaws, which means it can outrun, out-bite, and generally outlast almost all other animals. However, the wolf was eventually met with a potent rival – us. We humans (and our fellow travellers like mice and rats) have now surpassed wolves in our reach across the continents. In return, wolves have been driven out of much of their previous territories by farmers seeking to protect their livestock. Nevertheless, these tough dogs, the biggest of the 40 or so canine species, are still the most far-flung land carnivores on Earth, ranging from the icy fringes of the Arctic and cold northern forests to the arid shrublands of Africa and the mountains of Mexico. The wolf is excluded from South America, southern Africa, Southeast Asia and Australia by other dog species – although in this latter case, some authorities regard the Australian dingo as just another grey wolf subspecies. Being so widely spread in different habitats, local populations of wolves have evolved striking features. Although the picture is far from clear cut, a total of 38 subspecies of grey wolf have been identified, plus three wolf populations are deemed so distinct that they constitute separate species.

LEFT:

Grey wolf
Despite its name, the most common species of wolf is seen with fur ranging in colour from white to brown, red and jet black. The perception of grey hair is generally created by a mixture of hair colours.

Man's best friend
Every pet dog is a wolf in disguise, with some breeds being a lot further from the primordial wild form than others. Despite the big difference in appearance, all domestic dogs belong to the grey wolf species and could breed successfully with their wild cousins.

Eurasian wolf
If there is such a thing as a typical wolf, it is the Eurasian subspecies. This was the first type of grey wolf to be described, against which all other subspecies are compared. Grey with flecks of rusty red, this subspecies is found all the way from the Himalayas and the Siberian Pacific to Scandinavia.

PREVIOUS PAGE:
Eye to eye
Wolves are born with blue eyes, but these change to a golden yellow after about four months.

LEFT:
Timber wolf
The grey wolf also goes by the name 'timber wolf', referring to the species' close association with forest habitats. Without doubt, the chilly conifer forests of Canada and Siberia are the strongholds of today's wolf population.

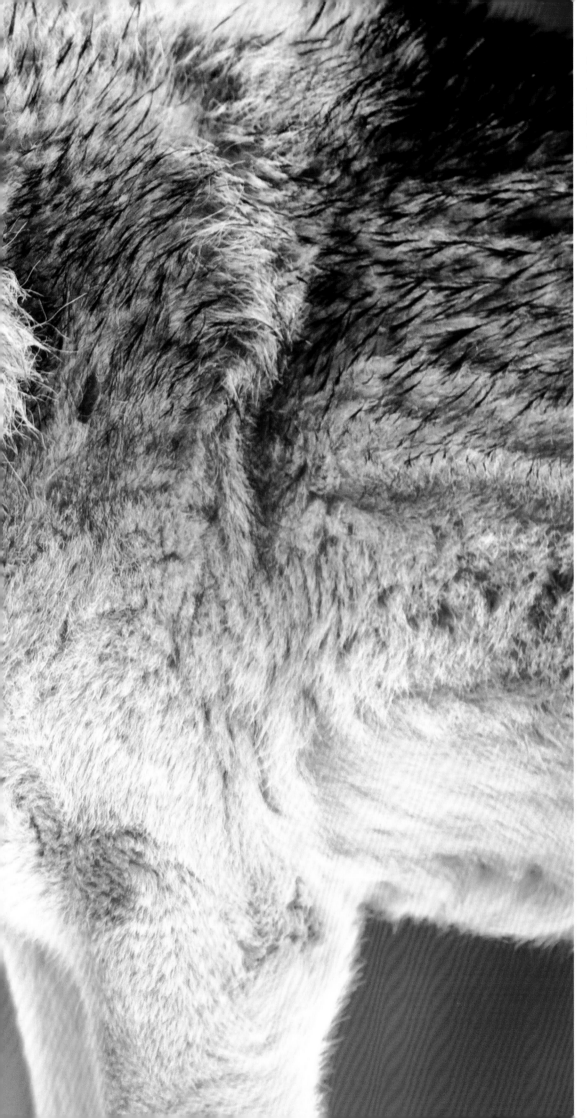

19

Sensory systems
Wolves have dichromatic vision where reds and greens both appear as the same colour. The animal has acute hearing, but its primary sense is smell, which is used to track prey, detect threats and pick up signals from pack mates.

ABOVE AND OPPOSITE TOP:
Northwestern wolf
Also known as the Mackenzie Valley wolf, this subspecies lives in western Canada and spreads into Alaska to the north and Washington State in the south. It is one of the largest of any wolf subspecies, with adult males regularly weighing in above 50kg (110lb). Northwestern wolves have a sturdier body and a more thick-set jaw than Eurasian wolves.

OPPOSITE BOTTOM:
Arctic wolf
Obviously characterized by its white fur, the Arctic wolf is a medium-sized subspecies that lives in the Canadian High Arctic, especially the Queen Elizabeth Islands, such as Ellesmere Island, and parts of Greenland. Up there, the wolf is hunting on ice caps for most of the year, with only a short thaw during the midsummer period.

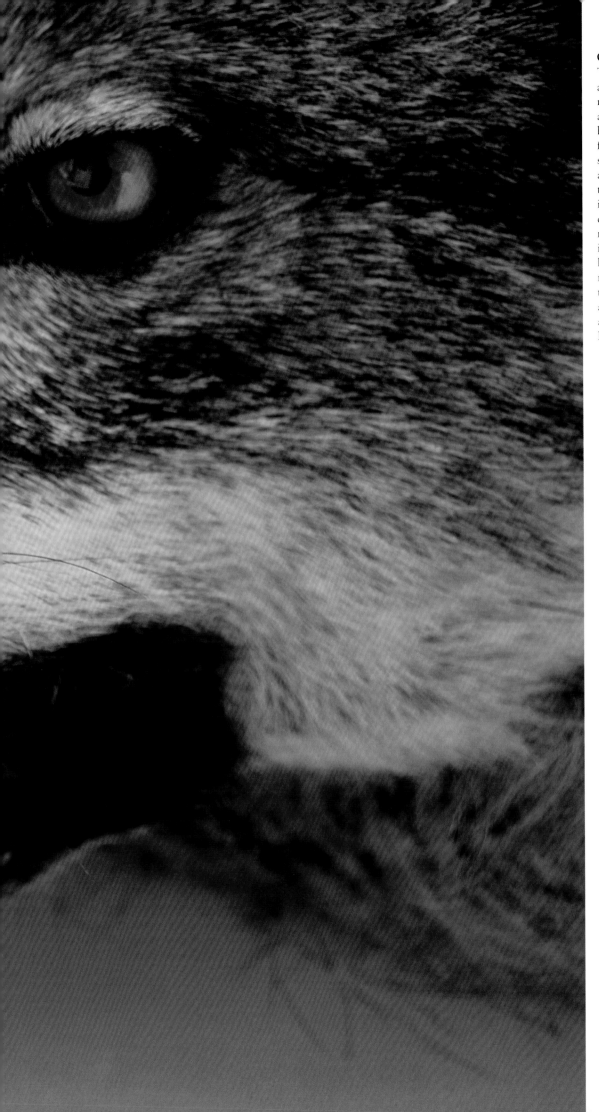

Canines

The wolf and the rest of the dogs and foxes belong to the family of mammals known as the Canidae and are often collectively described by the adjective 'canine'. The wolf, for example, is the biggest canine species. The terms Canidae, canid and canine all derive from 'canis', the Latin word for dog. This wolf is showing off its long fangs, better described as its canine teeth. The name of this type of tooth was inspired by the wolf and its allies, but it is used to describe the dental make-up of any mammal with these fang-like teeth. Cats, bears and other meat eaters have canines, as do humans, but rodents and herbivores, such as sheep, do not.

Yukon wolf

This subspecies of wolf, which varies in colour from a reddish tan to a pale grey, lives in the protected wildernesses of northwestern Canada and the interior of Alaska, including the Denali National Park. The subspecies is a strong contender for the biggest type of wolf on Earth. Males are regularly heavier than 50kg (110lb), and the largest verified specimen weighed in at 80kg (176lb), and there are unconfirmed reports of even heavier beasts.

Vancouver Island
The large island just off the southern coast of British Columbia is home to a particularly interesting population of wolves. Analysis of their DNA shows that these wolves are related to the first migration of wolves from eastern Asia (where the species arose around two million years ago). The wolves living in neighbouring regions on Canada are related to populations that arrived later.

LEFT:
Ethiopian wolf
Living in the isolated meadows of the Ethiopian Highlands, these dogs are designated as a separate species to the grey wolf. They survive on a near-exclusive diet of mole rats that live in burrows beneath the lush, rocky pastures. The species is classified as endangered not least because of the pressures placed on its mountain habitat by farmers, but also because of the presence of feral domestic dogs, which frequently interbreed with the wild wolves.

ABOVE:
Egyptian wolf
Once thought to be a species of golden jackal, this small dog is now known to belong to a separate species called the African golden wolf. Compared to the grey wolves of further north, this desert species relies much more on scavenging for foods such as carrion than hunting for fresh kills. Ancient Egyptian mythology owes much to this species, with Anubis, the god of the afterlife, sporting a wolf-like head.

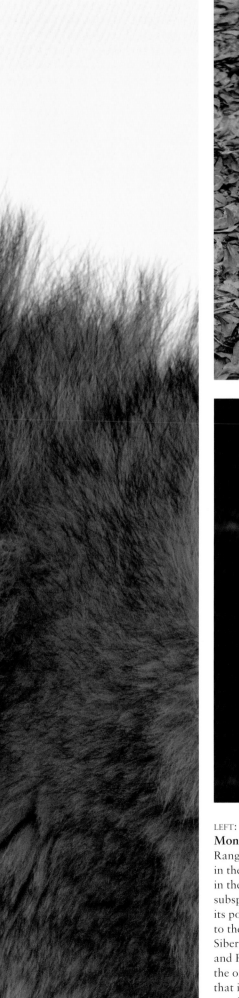

LEFT:

Mongolian wolf

Ranging from the Altai Mountains in the west to the Korean Peninsula in the east, this rugged, red-furred subspecies has actually expanded its population in recent years due to the human persecution of the Siberian tiger in northern China and Russia's Far East. This cat is the only Asian predator around that is big and fierce enough to stand up to a wolf pack.

ABOVE TOP:

Red wolf

A debate continues over whether the red wolves of the American South are an ancient species that predates the grey wolf or another subspecies. Another school of thought is that red wolves are hybrids of coyotes and grey wolves. Either way, the red wolf is critically endangered and thought to be extinct outside of protected areas.

ABOVE:

Eastern wolf

Also known as the Great Lakes wolf, this medium-sized subspecies of grey wolf lives in and around the St Lawrence River Valley. Genetic evidence suggests that the eastern wolf is 30 per cent coyote, which explains the relatively small average adult size. Being small means this wolf does not pose much of a threat to larger deer, such as moose and elk.

ABOVE:
Sensitive hearing
A wolf is alive to the comings and goings in its surroundings due to its sharp sense of hearing. It can hear high frequencies slightly beyond the scope of human hearing. The pinna or outer ear is manoeuvrable and swivels to capture the faintest sounds and pinpoint their likely direction.

OPPOSITE:
Howls
Few animal calls are as distinctive as the howl of a wolf. The howl is used for long-distance communication and can be heard over an area of 130 km^2 (50 mi^2). Distinct howls are used to call a pack to a fresh kill, bring in reinforcements during a chase, and to stake a claim on a territory.

Iberian wolf
Cut off from the rest of the wolf world by the Pyrenees mountain range, the Iberian wolves form the largest population of wild dogs in western Europe. They have a slighter build than their cousins who live in colder climes. They are easy to identify by the white patches on the upper lips.

Wild rovers
The latest surveys show that northern Spain has the highest concentration of wolves of any region in western Europe. Provinces such as Galicia, Asturias, Castile and Leon have seven wolves living in every 100 km² (39 mi²). The wolves are a protected species in Spain and Portugal but they are nevertheless still under a serious threat from illegal hunting.

Maned wolf

The grey wolf does not live south of the Equator (if we discount the Australian dingo as being a wolf subspecies, that is). South America has its own wolf species, the maned wolf, which lives in Brazil, Paraguay and Peru. The gangly anatomy of this species has seen it likened to a 'fox on stilts'. Its outlandishly long legs give it a height of about 1m (3ft), which helps it to see over the tops of tall grasses in its swampy pampas habitat.

OPPOSITE:

Distant relative

Despite the name, the maned wolf is only distantly related to other wolf species. Instead it is a closer cousin to the foxes and so belongs to the other side of the canid family. The family is very roughly split (with several exceptions) into two tribes: the vulpine dogs including the foxes, and the lupine species made up of the true wolves and their allies.

ABOVE:

Danger signal

When prepared for a fight, the mane wolf shows off how it won its name. A strip of dark hair that runs from the back of the head to the shoulders stands erect when the wolf detects a threat. Unlike the wolves of the north, the maned wolf is primarily solitary in nature and has to contend with more powerful predators, such as pumas and jaguars.

Arabian wolf

A strong contender for the smallest type of grey wolf, members of this desert subspecies are half as tall – around 60cm (2ft) – as their forest-living cousins and weigh little more than 20kg (44lb). It is just as likely to feed on carrion and human food waste as it is to hunt for itself. The wolf lives mostly in the Sinai Peninsula, Jordan and Iraq and the southern part of the Arabian Peninsula, especially Yemen.

OPPOSITE:
Arctic wolf
The white polar wolf is adapted
to life in cold temperatures. Its
muzzle and its ears are shorter to
reduce the risks of frostbite and
limit the amount of body heat
it sheds. The Arctic subspecies
also has thick fur on its feet and a
layer of fat under the skin to store
nutrients for lean times and to
provide an insulatory layer.

ABOVE:
Tundra wolf
This subspecies lives along the
northern fringes of Alaska and
Canada, where the deeper soils
are permanently frozen, meaning
that trees cannot put down roots.
Therefore, the land habitat is
dominated by treeless tundra. In
the coldest parts of winter, wolf
packs will retreat into the forests,
following their prey, such as
caribou and wapiti deer.

Ice hunter
Life is hard for the Arctic wolf, with winters bringing temperatures as low as −50°C (−50°F) and long periods of total darkness. While other subspecies tend to spend long periods alone in warmer periods, Arctic wolf packs are especially tight social units, where the members have to rely on each other for survival. Sources of food include lemmings, which burrow through the snow, musk oxen and Arctic hares.

PREVIOUS PAGE LEFT:

Tibetan wolf

This subspecies lives on either side of the Himalayas, spreading through Tibet into the rest of China and extending south into Nepal and India. The Tibetan wolf is characterized by a more pointed snout than other types and has a woolly coat to keep out the biting mountain winds.

PREVIOUS PAGE RIGHT:

Mexican wolf

Also known as the lobo, this subspecies is the smallest type of wolf in the Americas. Once spread over the original northern colonial territories of Mexico, the lobo is now highly endangered and persists in a few small pockets in the US state of New Mexico and the Sierra Madre Occidental in Mexico. Along with the Vancouver Island wolf, the Mexican subspecies represents the earliest kind of wolf to spread into the Americas from Siberia around 50,000 years ago.

LEFT:

African golden wolf

Until new DNA evidence was uncovered in 2015, these small African scavengers were classified as golden jackals. However, they now constitute their own species, living across the grassland and semi-desert regions of sub-Saharan Africa from Tanzania in the east to Senegal in the west. The range does not extend further south due to the presence of the African wild dog and two other jackal species that occupy that region.

PREVIOUS PAGE:
Dominance
Howling is risky for a lone wolf.
It is obvious to other wolves
nearby that the animal is alone,
and vulnerable to their attack. So
this wolf is secure in its position,
knowing that subordinate
members of its pack are nearby
to offer it protection.

LEFT:
Thickening fur
As autumn arrives, a wolf's coat
will thicken, with shorter, finer
hairs appearing beneath the longer
outer guard hairs, thus increasing
insulation for winter. Wolves living
in warmer climates have coarser
coats that protect the skin but
allow excess body heat to escape.

OPPOSITE:

Migrations

The wolf is a highly efficient mover and can cover several hundred kilometres in a matter of weeks. These kinds of journeys are made by young wolves who have been crowded out of their birth packs. They have no option but to move on, although the process of finding a new pack is fraught with risk.

OPPOSITE BOTTOM:

Play bow

It looks as if this steppe wolf, which lives in Central Asia, is having a good stretch. In fact it is performing a play bow, which is a signal to others that it is friendly and wants to play. Play will build familiarity and create a bond between the participants. A pack that plays together, stays together.

ABOVE:

Offensive look

This timber wolf is exuding confidence and dominance. The body from the ears down is standing tall, thereby maximizing height. The slight show of teeth signals exactly who is in charge to subordinates. If this wolf were put under threat by another wolf, it would have the backing of other pack members.

Defensive posture

The low, hunched posture with mouth open and teeth arrayed in a snarl is a signal that this wolf feels it is in danger and is ready to defend itself, most probably from the wolves in another pack who are attempting to force it out of a hunting territory. The attacking dogs will size up this foe, assessing its willingness to fight. If it can show enough aggression it may avoid actual combat.

Wolves in Winter

The wolf is a northern species, now more so than ever. Its historical range encompassed every land habitat in the Northern Hemisphere save the sand seas of the Sahara and similar bone-dry regions. The advent of human civilization inevitably saw this range shrink, as the wolf was pushed out of the more fertile and temperate regions and forced to take refuge in the cold and barren habitats of the distant north. Today's wolves are largely animals of the taiga, the great boreal forests that ring the Arctic zones of North America and Eurasia. Few wolf populations persist south of here, but a few do live even further north, where the conifer forests fade out into tundra, a treeless land where only the hardiest creatures survive.

The taiga and tundra are lands of near-perpetual winter, and all the wildlife living there – including the wolf – must be well prepared for cold weather. During its winter, the Northern Hemisphere is tilted away from the Sun. The star appears lower in the sky for shorter periods each day, and its light and heat arrive at a shallower angle and are less intense as a result. This effect grows as one heads north, and the North Pole famously receives no light at all for six months straight. The wolf contends with the rigours of the northern winter not just by adapting its physiology to stay warm, but also adopting complex social behaviours to maximize its chance of survival. When winter comes, the wolves are ready.

LEFT:

Weight advantage
Deep snow offers little challenge to the wolf. While heavier animals, including likely prey, such as boars and deer, will sink into the snow and struggle to move at speed, the lightweight wolf is able to spread its lower mass over a wider area – large paws help here – and extricate itself from the drifts with little difficulty.

Single file
After snow a pack will walk in single file, with the dominant male and
female taking it in turns to lead the way. This way of moving saves energy
because the lead dog clears the way for its followers.

First winter
Wolf cubs, born in the early summer, have been on the move with the pack since the autumn. By winter, they are well able to keep up with the adults, and even find time to play. This is a crucial activity that makes them strong and agile for hunting but also begins to lay the foundations of the future hierarchy within the pack.

ABOVE AND OPPOSITE:
Black wolf
The British Columbia wolf is the only grey wolf subspecies to be
consistently dark in colour – more a deep cinnamon than solid black.
The wolf lives along a narrow strip of the BC coast as far north as the
Alexander Archipelago in Alaska, and it is isolated from other wolves by
the Coast Mountains. The dark colouring offers no benefit in the snow,
but may reflect the way this subspecies hunts in rocky coastal and island
habitats for fish and other small prey.

Who's boss?
This grey wolf must rely on its pack mates for survival in the depths of winter. It is no top dog, and its body language is indicating that it is submitting to a more dominant pack member. The submissive posture includes a slight crouch, tail held down or curled under the body, and the head lowered with mouth held in a grin.

Scent signals
The wolf has little interest in the scent of this wild plant. Instead it is sniffing out signs of other wolves. It can identify friend from foe, stranger from familiar, potential mate or reproductive rival by the precise mingling of the scent left by passing wolves as sprays of urine, droppings, and even in footprints.

Constant vigilance
A wolf pack cannot hibernate through the winter, or become dormant in some other way. Its members are constantly patrolling the boundaries of the territory, refreshing scent marks with their collective smell and ensuring that a neighbouring pack, or a new set of incomers, is not taking advantage of its hunting grounds.

Checking status
To our eyes, these two European grey wolves are having fun in the snow, but in the context of a pack, every interaction is a power play that tests and perhaps reorders the hierarchy or reasserts a dominance. In wolf language, the underdog always makes itself lower, smaller and less threatening than the more senior pack member.

Hudson Bay wolf
In the icy winter it becomes impossible to tell where the ocean begins and the land ends. The wolf will need to know, because beyond the land the ice is home to polar bears hunting for seals. The two predators rarely meet, and give each other a wide berth when they do. However, as global warming takes its toll, bears in this part of Canada are being pushed further into wolf territory in search of food.

ABOVE:

Double layer

A wolf's coat is made up of two distinct layers of hair. The underfur is short, fine and dense, and this serves as insulation. Longer guard hairs have a protective waterproofing function, and in the case of these tundra wolves are fine and glossy to trap a further layer of insulating air against the skin like a lightweight but warm blanket.

OPPOSITE:

Going grey

The colour of a wolf's hair does follow a pattern, with paler animals living in more monochrome habitats, such as deserts and snow-covered tundra. However, most grey wolves use a disruptive mixture of colours so they can have a better chance of moving unseen against the complex backdrop of rock, snow and vegetation.

Standing proud
A dominant wolf shows off his prowess with his tall, straight-legged stance. His thick, woolly winter fur is also erect to give the illusion of size and make him look even more impressive. Submissive animals flatten their fur as a clear visual signal of their place in the dominance hierarchy.

ABOVE:

Stay back

This Arctic wolf is showing off its physical attributes, but it is in a defensive posture that aims to fend off the advance of another pack. The mouth is open and the tongue is retracted to show off the teeth, but the ears are folded backward and the head is held low to indicate that the wolf is standing its ground and not trying to muscle in on another pack's territory.

OPPOSITE TOP:

Staking a claim

A pack of wolves stand on the frozen Wapiti Lake in Yellowstone National Park in Wyoming and call together to alert any other wolves in the area to their presence. In winter, packs and lone wolves are often forced to travel beyond their territories to find adequate food supplies. As a result, resident packs frequently assert their territorial claims.

OPPOSITE BOTTOM:

Smelling prey

In polar regions, animal life continues unabated beneath the frozen surface, with voles and lemmings moving through tunnel networks dug in the snow. Arctic wolves rely on these rodents as a source of winter food, and use their sense of hearing and smell to locate these prey as they scurry around unseen.

LEFT:

Rest period
Wolves are most active at night, when they take advantage of the dark to move unseen in their search for hunting grounds. Night movements are especially long and arduous in winter; and during the day, the animals hunker down for a well-earned rest.

NEXT PAGE LEFT:

Cold feet
The blood vessels in the wolf's feet work as an efficient heat exchanger. Cold blood from the feet meets warmer blood from the body in the ankle, where the colder blood is heated up by the warm blood – which in turn is cooled. The result is that the wolf's feet are always very cold, barely above freezing in winter, so very little valuable body heat is lost to the ground but instead redirected back into the body.

NEXT PAGE RIGHT:

Skin control
The wolf's skin is at work controlling temperature. In the cold, the blood vessels in the skin are contracted, reducing the amount of heat that reaches the body surface. This minimizes the amount of heat lost to the air during cold conditions.

Mountain habitats
It is not just the Arctic and timber wolves of northern habitats that must contend with cold winters. These Iberian wolves live in mountainous regions, where the high altitude means the air is too thin to hold much heat. Winters are often bitterly cold here too.

Rapid transit
Wolves have longer legs than other wild dog species. This helps them to run that bit faster. The longer legs also offer an important advantage when navigating through soft snow. At full speed, a wolf can jump 5m (16.4ft) in a single bound.

Panting

Wolves can maintain high speeds for long periods, and the body gets hot even during the winter. Wolves cannot sweat nearly as much as a human can, so they shed heat by panting instead. The process is largely the same; excess heat energy is released from the body by making water evaporate from the damp tongue dangling from the mouth.

PREVIOUS PAGE:
Hello again!
Pack mates greet a member who
has just rejoined the group by
swimming across a river. The new
arrival gets some friendly nips
on the back of the neck by more
dominant dogs as a welcome back
into the team.

RIGHT:
Fresh water
The frozen winter landscape is
actually a very dry place, with less
liquid water available than during
summer. This wolf is quenching
its thirst by licking the ice covering
the surface of a frozen lake.

Siberian survivor

The tundra wolf of Eurasia lives along the treeless coasts of the Arctic Ocean. This subspecies is the likely ancestor of the last wave of wolves to spread eastward from Asia into North America. They have pale coats like the American polar subspecies but also have a reddish tinge to their outer guard hairs covering the grey underfur beneath.

Rolling deep
There is strength in numbers, and wolf packs spend more time in tight-knit groups during the winter than during the summer. The pack is more reliant on large prey, which they kill as a team, in winter, and are more likely to meet another pack. Attacks are an ever-present threat.

Border clash
A wolf pack must defend its territory. Without it, the pack cannot find food, cannot produce young and will be forced to disband. The pack will patrol the border regularly; if it encounters outsiders then its members have no choice but to attack. Up to a fifth of all wolf deaths occur during these inter-pack battles.

Sit it out
It is not possible to hunt during bad winter weather, and the only option for the wolf is to wait it out. The thick fur is able to withstand temperatures as low as -40°C (-40°F) with little difficulty. However, the wolf cannot go without food for more than a couple of weeks.

LEFT:

Looking for territory

Young adult wolves have little future in a large successful pack, so they set out on their own, covering hundreds of kilometres to find a new place to live. A lone male teams up with a lone female from a neighbouring pack, and they set off in winter to seek out their own territory.

ABOVE:

Into the wind

As well as low temperatures, wolves in the High Arctic must contend with strong wind. Wind does not make temperatures go lower, but it does increase the rate at which a wolf will lose heat. To mitigate this effect, the wolf sits with its face into the wind, minimizing the area of the body that is exposed.

OPPOSITE TOP:

Midwest relic

The dark wolves of Minnesota represent a relict population, or a pocket of wolves with an ancient heritage. They are believed to have moved to this part of North America during the last ice age. Most of the wolves in North America today are descended from wolves that arrived from East Asia several thousand years later.

OPPOSITE BOTTOM:

Long-distance life

The winter is a nomadic phase for many packs. An Arctic pack, with a large, barren territory, will move up to 200 km (124 mi) every night in the search for food and shelter. The ultra-efficient wolf can trot along for many hours on end.

ABOVE:

Keep moving

Boreal, meaning 'northern', land habitats have a smaller capacity than warmer ones to the south. Put simply, there is less light and warmth so food of any kind is spread more thinly over the area. For an apex predator, such as the wolf, its prey are especially widely dispersed. These wolves may have to walk for days on end to find their next meal.

The Wolf Pack

The pack is one of the most fascinating social groups in the animal kingdom. It is based around a single breeding pair, the alphas. Other members of the pack are mostly this pair's sons and daughters of various ages, plus maybe some brothers, sisters and members of the more extended family. Typically a pack contains about a dozen adult wolves plus a litter of the cubs, but groups have been found with more than 40 members. Like any close-knit family, a wolf pack is a fractious place. Every member takes its position in a rigorous hierarchy, with the beta dogs protecting the alphas, in the hope of succeeding them one day, all the way down to the omegas, who are bottom of the heap. Wolves with no prospect of reaching top-dog status, generally young adults born into overcrowded packs, are hounded out by the antisocial behaviour of their superiors. The lone wolves set off to start their own pack. It is rare for itinerant wolves to be accepted into a foreign pack, so instead a wandering male and female from two unrelated packs will pair up and search out a place free from other wolves. Their wolf family may go on to hold its new territory for many generations. Wolf society has many parallels with that of humans, and it is likely that the two species lived alongside each other for much of their early history. Already sharing an understanding of how to live in families, wild wolves became the pet dogs that have joined our society – or perhaps we joined theirs.

Leading figures
When a wolf pack is on the move, it is the alphas that decide when they leave, where the pack will go, and the pair take it in turns to lead the way.

Multiple harmony
A pack calls together to signal its strength in numbers and reinforce its claim over a territory. The lead wolf calls first and other pack members respond in a jarring harmony of rising howls. The multiplex of sounds makes it difficult to count the number of animals, so any other wolves within earshot will opt for caution and steer clear.

Maintaining the order
Although a model of animal cooperation, a wolf pack is not wholly harmonious. Members are constantly being tested by more lowly wolves trying to rise up the ranks and such subordination must be dealt with quickly. To that end, this wolf is signalling its dominance, and a willingness to hold its place in the pack by force, by wrinkling its forehead and baring its teeth in a snarl.

ABOVE:
Play-fight

Not every encounter between wolves is a threat of violence. Pack members play together even in adulthood to reinforce bonds of trust – and solidify rankings. The dominant dog's head is always above that of a subordinate as a clear signal of each other's rank.

OPPOSITE:
Band of brothers and sisters

Working together has obvious advantages, but there are disadvantages, too. Many wolves will never have offspring of their own yet must put their lives on the line to feed the cubs of the alpha pair. The only reason they do this is because they share a genetic relationship with the alphas, and thus benefit in a small way from their leaders' success.

Size limits
The optimal size of a wolf pack is about 12 adults. Such a pack is big enough to control a territory that is large enough to supply food for all, and includes a border zone where the pack will rarely hunt, but keep clear of other wolves. A smaller pack will struggle to sweep clear a safe space, while a bigger one is too fragile to stay together as it is riven by frequent squabbles over status.

LEFT:
Relaxing summer
The summer is a stationary period for the pack. They have set up a den in the heartland of their territory in order to raise young, and wolves will hunt alone or in pairs for smaller animals that are more common in summer. In winter, the pack will go back to a life on the move.

Small and quiet

The Indian wolf subspecies is the closest relative of the jackal. This little south Asian wolf generally hunts alone for rodents and hares. It forms a pair to take down antelopes, with one wolf distracting the prey while the partner lunges in from behind. The Indian wolf gathers into bigger packs in order to defend carrion finds, similar to the jackal. Some authorities suggest that the Indian wolf should be classified as a separate species.

OPPOSITE TOP:
Playful grin
Just as a smile carries the opposite message of a snarl, these dogs are in a more playful mood, indicated by their broad, flat foreheads.

OPPOSITE BOTTOM:
A close bond
A clear hierarchy, rigidly enforced, builds strong bonds between the members of a pack. They trust each other to behave in cooperative ways.

ABOVE:
Submission
An omega wolf will signal its low status and placate the top dog by approaching with its head lowered and licking the chief's nose.

Domination
The alpha female is superior to all other members of the pack except the alpha male, who tends to be larger and stronger.

Warning signs
Cooperation has fallen apart as
this African wolf (right) defends
a carcass from another wolf by
taking a highly defensive posture
that shows it is ready to fight to
keep control of the food supply.

Team players
A wolf pack is only as strong as its weakest member. If all wolves work together, the pack will prosper to the benefit of all members.

PREVIOUS PAGE:
Lazy days
During the stationary phase in summer, wolves will spend most of the days resting near the den. As well as building up reserves for lean times to come, the lounging wolves act as able guards for the pack's new litter of cubs.

LEFT:
Morning call
The wolf's howl is not simply a way of declaring ownership of a territory and thus avoiding unnecessary clashes with the neighbours. It is also a way that the pack shows solidarity and builds bonds between its members.

136

OPPOSITE:
Final option
When wolves meet strangers there is generally a fight to the death. To avoid such encounters, a wolf pack puts time and energy into controlling its territory through scent marks, group calls and regular patrols.

ABOVE:
Stability
The orderly society of wolves is what allows the animal to succeed in habitats with cold temperatures and long winters. These Yukon wolves are able to rest in summer thanks to their habitat-beating social structure.

PREVIOUS PAGE:
Home team
Ethiopian wolves hunt alone, but
live in packs of six or more adults.
All pack members are female
except a breeding male, who mates
with a single breeding female – or
with a female from a neighbouring
pack. Most males are banished to
a life alone.

RIGHT:
On the look-out
One of the driving forces that
pushes animals to live in groups
is the pooling of defences.
Working together, nothing gets
past a pack of wolves. Any
animal approaching the area will
be spotted by at least one pack
member, who warns the others
with a bark.

PREVIOUS PAGE:
In step
During the winter nomadic phase, the wolf pack moves constantly from dusk until dawn. The wolves generally travel at an average speed of about 8km/h (5mph), which is the speed of a human jog.

LEFT:
Local knowledge
The pack knows every patch of its territory. Scent marks are left at obvious landmarks like rocks and tree stumps throughout the area, and are regularly freshened up during pack patrols.

NEXT PAGE:
Busy winter
When cold temperatures drive small prey, such as rodents and hares, into hibernation, the pack gets on the move to find larger prey that must be hunted in teams.

ABOVE:

Taking the scent

Wolves live in a world of scent, and smell their pack mates after a period apart. This reinforces the shared bond between them and also reveals which other dogs their friends have been in contact with, further building a sense of belonging among pack members.

OPPOSITE TOP:

Young guns

The younger members of a pack have a choice. They can leave to start their own pack, a high risk and high reward strategy that sees them and their offspring dominating a pack for generations. Otherwise they can stay at home and climb to the top rank, a safe but unlikely option.

OPPOSITE BOTTOM:

Old hands

Older members of a pack are not given much reprieve as they get weaker and less able. A stronger, fitter beta dog will drive them out of the pack and take their place as soon as he or she senses the opportunity to do so.

Submissive behaviour
The lowly members of the pack work just as hard at signalling their harmlessness as dominant ones do to make it clear how tough they are. Many submissive behaviours see one wolf open themselves up to the possibility of attack. They roll on their backs to expose their bellies and they place their snouts next to their master's jaws, licking the chin, nose and gums.

Sound of the howl
A male wolf howls with a distinct 'oh' sound that starts very deep and rises by an octave. Female wolves' howls sound more like an 'oo' that is less deep than the male's.

PREVIOUS PAGE:

Greetings

These wolves are pleased to see each other. There appears to be no conflict between them as to their relative dominance, and so the tails are held in a neutral position, with the legs bent and bodies relaxed.

ABOVE:

Territorial hideouts

A river often marks a boundary of a wolf pack's territory. Wolves are good swimmers but packs would avoid crossing a river en masse in summer. However, in winter the water may freeze, allowing the pack – or portions of it – to spread into new areas.

OPPOSITE:

Group scent

Every wolf has a unique scent, and together these smells of a pack combine to make a group scent. These scents are created by several wolves marking in the same places.

Rough and tough
A pack makes life easier for a wolf, but their life is still very hard and often short. Attacking large prey carries a risk of serious injury, and the pack will not – cannot – wait for a hurt member to recover. Only the toughest and luckiest wolves will make it.

The Hunt

A wolf is the outstanding land predator on Earth. It is not as big and fierce as a bear or tiger, but the wolf's ability to adapt, to use cunning as well as strength and speed, to work as a team or to kill alone, sets it apart and allows it to live in nearly all kinds of land habitat, save tropical forests. The world's wolves have carved out many different ways of life that see them catching fish from rivers, snatching food from lions, pouncing on lemmings buried under snow, and bringing down moose ten times their size. Of course, the hunting prowess of wolves is what has led to its relative downfall as farmers drive the packs from much of their original habitat. The wolf kills with its teeth, but this is not its primary weapon. As well as being equipped with good night vision, sensitive hearing and an acute sense of smell (although not nearly as good as that of an artificially bred bloodhound), the wolf's most deadly dimension is its stamina. Although it can run fast, a wolf cannot out-sprint and overtake a sprightly and nervous prey like a deer. However, it can give chase for several hours – not always at top speed but in a dogged pursuit that harries the victim constantly. Eventually, the prey is too exhausted to go any further and helpless in the face of relentless attacks by the circling pack. Wolves kill big prey slowly but steadily, taking bites from the face and belly until the victim collapses from blood loss. Wasting no time, the pack begins to gorge on the fresh food – so fresh, in fact, that the prey is eaten alive!

LEFT:
Bite and slice
The wolf's fangs grip flesh as the front incisors cut out a mouthful of food. Wolves do not have flat molar teeth for grinding food. Instead the back teeth are scissor-like carnassials which that bones and slice up meat making it ready for swallowing.

Bothering sheep
Livestock farming, with its mild, tame animals bred to stay herded together, is a gift to wolf packs. Sheep are especially easy pickings for wolves. Shepherds have traditionally kept tame working dogs to ward off wolf attacks, taking advantage of a pack's natural caution about moving into territory controlled by other dogs.

Stand-off
A large elk stag, equipped with a formidable set of spiked antlers, eyes a pair of wolves. The pack has forced the deer to the bottom of a valley, far from the relative safety of the trees further up the hill. Now the wolves block the deer's path to safety while other wolves make their way around behind and go in for the kill.

The chase
Wolves do not catch and kill large prey quickly. Instead they give chase, waiting for their victim to tire. A wolf has a top speed of about 55km/h (34mph). This is not quite as fast as its prey, but the wolf can maintain high speeds for longer – about 20 minutes – and can travel at a slower run for hours on end.

PREVIOUS PAGE LEFT:
Scavenging

This lead wolf is smart enough to not pass up the opportunity of an easy meal and has scavenged the remains of a dead animal. Scavenging carrion like this is a more common behaviour among wolves in drier habitats.

PREVIOUS PAGE RIGHT:
Fast food

When it is time to eat, a wolf has no time to spare and it eats as fast as it possibly can. The pack will not share out meals fairly; it is first come, first served.

RIGHT:
Running

All dogs, and especially wolves, are engines for running over long distances – to find food and chase down prey. The long legs give a long stride, and the body is slim and lightweight bar the large thorax, which holds big lungs and a heart that is twice as big as another mammal of a similar length and weight.

Big heads
Compared to its slender and agile body, the wolf's head appears very large. The neck and shoulders carry large muscles for holding up the heavy skull. The skull has a large parietal bone stretching back behind the eye where the powerful jaw muscles are attached.

OPPOSITE TOP:

Mole rat diet

Unlike its cosmopolitan cousins, the Ethiopian wolf has a very limited diet, restricted almost entirely to mole rats that live in burrows under the highland meadows of the wolf's home. They hunt alone; a pack would be a positive hindrance for catching such little prey.

OPPOSITE BOTTOM:

Dogged pursuit

While chasing prey, the pack will try to force their victim into a place from which they cannot escape, such as a river, a steep ravine or the slippery surface of a frozen lake.

BELOW:

Fishing

Wolves in Alaska and Canada collect the carcasses of salmon that die after breeding in rivers. Some packs also spend many hours watching for live salmon, which they snatch from the water with their jaws.

PREVIOUS PAGE:
Size difference
A pack of Arctic wolves attack a herd of musk oxen, a large relative of sheep adapted for life in polar regions. The wolves target the slowest musk ox and will chase, nip and pester it until it cannot defend itself from a final assault.

ABOVE:
Rendezvous
In summer, the cubs are carried to a rendezvous site, an open space close to a water supply and with well-marked boundaries, where the rest of the pack can meet up after lone hunting forays.

OPPOSITE TOP:
Meal for one
Wolves will hunt alone for small prey such as ground squirrels and hares. Solitary hunting means that the wolf does not have to share its meal with fellow pack members, although small prey have far less flesh on the bone.

OPPOSITE BOTTOM:
Left overs
This African wolf did not kill this zebu (an African domestic cow) but will claim it as its own nevertheless. The pack system here is used more to defend scavenged carcasses than for hunting.

PREVIOUS PAGE:

Dangerous times

Once the pack has cornered its prey, such as this American bison, the hunt enters its most dangerous phase. The 400kg (880lb) bison is going to fight back with kicking hooves and goring horns, which are more than capable of killing a wolf.

RIGHT:

Fast pounce

Fish do not fight back when hunted, but they require a great deal of time and energy to catch. This British Columbian wolf cannot resist giving it a go at some rapids deep in the forest as thousands of plump fish swim upstream to spawn.

LEFT:

Coastal life

Salmon are a valuable source of food for the packs in the Coast Range mountains of western Canada. In autumn, many thousands of dead fish pile up in shallow streams.

ABOVE TOP:

Grab and run

This Arabian wolf has got hold of a good meal from a carcass rotting in the desert. It has opted to run off with a personal supply to eat alone rather than try to defend the larger carcass from jackals and vultures.

ABOVE:

Stalking

With its ears focused forward to pick up the slightest sound of its prey rummaging in a shallow burrow, the Ethiopian wolf edges forward. When it is close enough it will lie in wait, ready to pounce on the mole rat when it comes to the mouth of its burrow.

Rip and slice
Wolves are not fussy eaters and make do with whatever they can kill. Their 42 teeth are adapted to extract as much from a carcass as possible, and can even crush up smaller bones to get at the marrow inside.

Exhausted prey
The end is near for this bison. It is bleeding from multiple attacks from the pack over the course of two days, and now is too weak to attempt to escape. The wolf pack will gather for the final onslaught.

Wolf Cubs

Born into a litter of at least five and perhaps as many as three times that number, a wolf cub begins life in a hidden den kept warm by its mother, the alpha female. Outside, the alpha male and the rest of the pack are keeping the den safe from attack. Weighing just 500g (17oz) when newborn, the cub is blind and largely hairless for the first 15 days of life. Then its eyes open, showing the distinctive blue that will eventually fade into the adult yellow iris. The growing cub, now able to see, begins to move around its home. However, only its front legs work at this stage, and the cub is not able to walk until it reaches about a month old. Even so, the cub will stay in the den for another month or more, and its mother will

rarely leave her young unattended in that time. She feeds them milk for about seven weeks, and in that time their diet is supplemented by food brought to the den by other pack members and regurgitated for them to eat. After weaning, the pack supplies their youngest members with scraps of meat. At the age of ten weeks, all cubs will be out of the den, exploring the surroundings under the watchful gaze of their elders. It is midsummer by now, and the cubs spend the long days play-fighting and following older wolves on hunts. They have never been left alone for a second, and already the cubs are asserting dominance through play as they take their place in a hierarchy. The cub that rules the playground may one day rule the pack.

Maned wolf
A maned wolf cub lives in a much smaller family than its grey wolf cousins. The mother of the cub does most of the rearing by herself, although the father brings food to the den on occasion. Maned wolf cubs generally born in late spring, spend one winter with their mother. Come their first birthday the litter of young wolves will leave home to build a life of their own.

PREVIOUS PAGE:
Protection
As an adult this wolf cub will have no natural enemies, but now it needs protection. It is most at risk from attack by brown bears and eagles. Hiding under an adult is good protection from the latter.

LEFT:
Den
Wolf cubs are born in a secluded den under a fallen tree or rock or in a cave, always located well inside the central region of the pack's territory. An alpha female will generally return to the same den to give birth to all of her litters.

ABOVE TOP:
Out and about
A wolf cub is able to walk from the age of about 20 days. This little guy has come to look around outside the den soon after learning to walk, but most cubs will not emerge from the den until they are at least two months old. Even then they are too small to go far.

ABOVE:
Teaching
Wolf cubs learn from the older members of the pack. Lessons include how to greet and interact with other members of the pack and how to respond to danger.

RIGHT:
Weapon system
The wolves have a full set of milk teeth, including canines, from the age of about one month. This allows them to eat solid foods supplied by their father and other pack members.

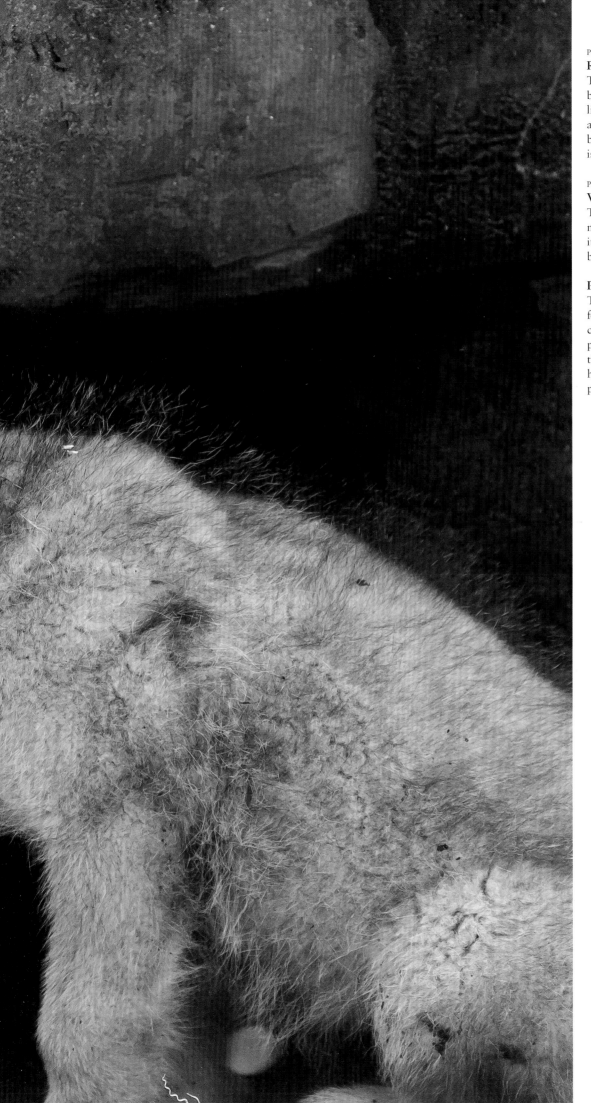

PREVIOUS PAGE LEFT:
Ready for escape
This gangly wolf cub looks to
be all ears. Even at this age it is
listening out for the sounds of
approaching danger and will dash
back to the security of the den if it
is spooked by anything.

PREVIOUS PAGE RIGHT:
Weight gain
The cub grows fast, putting on
muscle. By the age of four months
it will be 30 times heavier than its
birth weight of 500g (17oz).

Play-fight
The urge to play begins in the
fourth week of life, even before the
cubs have left the den. These early
play-fights are a test of strength
that will form the basis of the social
hierarchy that will be a constant
part of the wolves' adult lives.

ALL ON THIS PAGE:

Mothering

The cubs' mother, the alpha female, seldom leaves her litter for the first few months of the cubs' lives. She will retrieve cubs that have wandered too far from the den, feed them their first food as milk, and show them how to form the strong social bounds they'll need to live in a pack.

PREVIOUS PAGE:
Suckling wolf
A female wolf has ten teats, which is generally enough to suckle the cubs in a litter all at once. In big litters it is likely that one or more cub will starve to death.

RIGHT:
Preparing for winter
Cubs are born in late spring and need to be ready to move with the pack when winter hits. During autumn these Greenland wolves are developing a thick, woolly coat to keep out the extreme cold of their first winter.

PREVIOUS PAGE:
Life outside
Once all the cubs are strong enough to leave the den, they will move to a life outdoors, joining the rest of the pack. They learn about adult life by watching the grown-up wolves interacting as they come and go on hunting trips.

RIGHT:
Top dogs
After a few weeks of play-fighting, the cubs begin to fight for real, giving bites that are meant to hurt. A hierarchy is established in the first few months of life, with a distinct set of ranks for both male and female cubs.

Staying close
A cub will not stray far from its
mother or other pack members,
and dashes back to the den at the
first sign of trouble. Away from the
protection of the pack, the wolf
cub is at risk of attack from bears,
wild cats, birds of prey and snakes.

214

OPPOSITE LEFT:

Late arrival

The timing of a wolf's birth can be crucial. This dark cub was born late in the season, and now has a lot of growing to do before it is strong enough to travel with the pack during its winter wander.

OPPOSITE BOTTOM:

Paying respect

Cubs spend the summer learning how to fit in with the other members of the pack. When the winter arrives, the cubs will still be relying on the older members to keep them alive.

ABOVE:

Adolescent

In the autumn, the cub is big enough to join in with a hunt, first for small prey and then for larger, more dangerous foe. The risks of injury are high for the inexperienced hunter.

Alpha pair
All cubs in a pack have one mother, and she and the alpha male are likely to be the parents of most of the wolves, young and adult, in the pack. The pair only mate with each other.

Summer fun
A cub's first summer is filled with long lazy days, where it can romp in the sunshine with its brothers and sisters. All the food the cubs need is brought to them by their parents and other pack members.

Frozen ground
Arctic wolves live in areas where the ground is permanently frozen. In such a habitat, denning sites are in short supply. Packs will have used the same dens for centuries.

Life ahead
Most wild wolves live for about six years, and die from injuries or starvation. However, the lucky few will make it to an age of 13 or more.

Rocky ground

Mongolian wolves live in open grasslands and make their dens in rocky areas. Their future on the Mongolian steppe is uncertain because so many of the wild herbivores, such as antelope, that they used to prey on have now been replaced by domestic livestock – which is too risky to hunt.

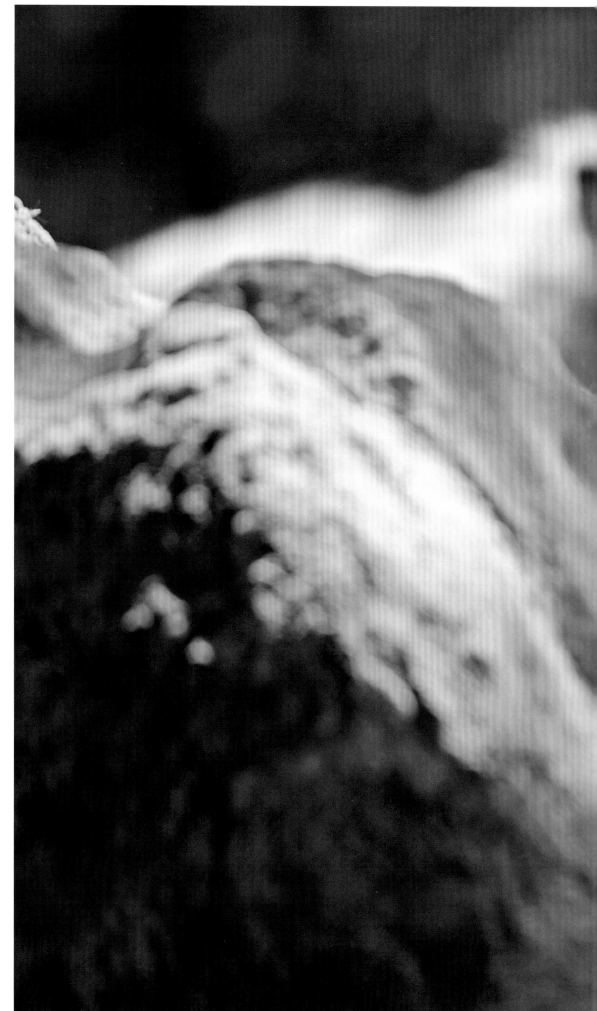

BELOW:
Off we go
This young wolf is raring to get started on its life with the pack. However, its life will be very hard going. In the lean times, it may have to eat the remains of its dead pack mates to ward off starvation.

OPPOSITE:
Taking its place
A wolf cub shows who is boss by submissively licking the chin of an older, wiser, and considerably tougher wolf. If it plays to its strengths, however, and picks its battles, this little cub might one day rule over a pack of its own.

Picture Credits